VETERANS DAY

BY MARLENE TARG BRILL

ILLUSTRATIONS BY QI Z. WANG

On My Own

HOLIDAYS

Carolrhoda Books, Inc./Minneapolis

This book is available in two editions:
Library binding by Carolrhoda Books, Inc., a division of Lerner Publishing Group
Soft cover by First Avenue Editions, an imprint of Lerner Publishing Group
241 First Avenue North
Minneapolis, MN 55401 U.S.A.

Website address: www.lernerbooks.com

Library of Congress Cataloging-in-Publication Data

Brill, Marlene Targ.
    Veterans Day / by Marlene Targ Brill ; illustrations by Qi Z. Wang.
        p.   cm. — (On my own holidays)
    ISBN: 1–57505–699–2 (lib. bdg. : alk. paper)
    ISBN: 1–57505–766–2 (pbk. : alk. paper)
    1. Veterans Day. 2. Holidays. I. Wang, Qi Z., ill. II. Title. III. Series.
D671.B75 2005
394.264—dc22   2004014800

Manufactured in the United States of America
1 2 3 4 5 6 – DP – 10 09 08 07 06 05

To children everywhere who celebrate peace —M.T.B.

To my mom, JiaMo, and my husband, Nardu,
who always encourage me —Q.W.

Each year on November 11, Americans
young and old march in parades.
Bands play national songs.

U.S. flags wave from homes, buildings,
and flagpoles.

What is everyone celebrating?

People in the United States
celebrate the holiday
Veterans Day every year.
We show veterans
how much they mean to us.
But who are veterans?
What makes them so special?
Veterans are people who have worked
to keep the United States safe and free.
They protected the land and seas
where we live.
They also protected ideas, people,
and places that are important
to the United States around the world.

Veterans come from different branches, or groups, of the U.S. armed forces. The branches include the army, navy, marines, air force, and coast guard. People in the armed forces are called servicepeople. Servicepeople work on land, at sea, and in the air. Each branch has a different job. People in the navy and coast guard sail ships that police our lakes and oceans. People in the air force fly planes that protect against attack from the air. People in the army go wherever they are needed on land. And the marines work at sea, in the air, and on the land.

Servicepeople's jobs often
put them in danger.
Sometimes they must fight in wars.
Other times, they help people in trouble,
such as after a bad storm
or plane crash.
They can get hurt or killed on the job.

3 1833 04061 4669

Many jobs keep servicepeople away
from home for a long time.
They miss their friends and families.
They give up their lives at home
so we can live in peace.
Veterans Day says thank you
to the men and women who give up
so much to help protect us.

The idea for Veterans Day
goes back to 1918.
This was a time before talking movies,
television, and jet planes.
World War I had ended
after four years of fighting.
The war had started when some
countries wanted more land and power.
These countries attacked their neighbors
to get the land and power they wanted.

The United States entered the war in 1917.
Almost 5 million Americans fought.
About 116,000 died.
On November 11, 1918,
the long, terrible war ended.
The last soldiers laid down their weapons.
The time was eleven o'clock
on the eleventh day
of the eleventh month of the year.

The end of fighting was called
an armistice.
News about the armistice
spread quickly.
People poured into streets
around the world.
Whistles blew and stores closed.
Everybody danced and hugged with joy
to have peace at last.

A year later, President
Woodrow Wilson asked Americans
to remember the armistice for one day.
He named November 11 Armistice Day.
At eleven o'clock, people
in the United States and other countries
stood silently for two minutes.
Staying silent was their way
to give thanks for peace.
The quiet time gave them a chance
to think about veterans
who helped win the peace.

Some nations wanted to do more
to remember their servicepeople.
In 1920, Britain and France each buried
a soldier in a special place of honor.
Nobody knew who the soldiers were.
The unknown soldiers stood for
all those who had died.
The British soldier was buried
with kings and queens.

Each sundown, French soldiers
lit a flame over their soldier's grave.
People in the United States got an idea.
Why not honor an unknown American
soldier the same way?

In 1921, an unknown soldier
was placed in a tomb,
a building for holding the dead.
The tomb was built in Arlington
National Cemetery in Virginia.
This is a special cemetery where people
who helped the United States
are buried.
Some of the dead are presidents.
Others are soldiers.
The Tomb of the Unknown Soldier
was shut at eleven o'clock
on November 11.
President Warren G. Harding
ordered people to fly flags halfway
down their flagpoles to show respect.

Americans liked having a place
they could visit to honor veterans.
But they wanted November 11
to be a national holiday.
A national holiday would give
everyone in the country
time to think about veterans.

Many people sent letters to lawmakers about their idea. The next president, Calvin Coolidge, said government buildings had to fly U.S. flags on November 11. He invited schools and churches to celebrate veterans. By then, 27 states had set aside November 11 as a state holiday.

In 1938, the nation's lawmakers
voted to make November 11
a national holiday.
It was a day to celebrate world peace.
Schools, banks, and
government buildings closed.
No mail came to homes or stores.
Towns held parades where scouts
and servicepeople marched.
Lawmakers kept the name
Armistice Day.
They wanted people to remember
World War I.

On the first national Armistice Day,
President Franklin D. Roosevelt
did something new.
He placed a circle of flowers
on the Tomb of the Unknown Soldier.
Other flowers came
from all over the country.
Soldiers who stood guard
shot their guns into the air.
One soldier played taps,
a song to honor the dead,
on a bugle.
Every president since 1938
has laid flowers on the tomb
and heard taps on November 11.

Three years later, the United States
entered another world war.
Once again, many nations battled
over land and power.
America sent more than 16 million
brave servicepeople to fight
in World War II.
Most came home unhurt.
But more than 400,000
died during the war.

Then another war raged in Korea
from 1950 to 1953.
People all over the country talked about
ways to show respect for servicepeople
from these wars too.

A man named Al King
decided to do something.
His nephew had died in World War II.
He had seen many young people
leave home to fight in Korea.
He knew many of them would be killed.
King ran a shoe store in Emporia, Kansas.

He fixed shoes of veterans
and their families for free.
He helped send food and clothes
to children of veterans.
Then in 1952, he asked townspeople
to set aside November 11 for all veterans.
He wanted to change the name
of the holiday to Veterans Day.

The idea caught on.

The next year, Emporia celebrated

the first Veterans Day with a parade.

Kansas governor Edward Arn gave a speech.

He said, "This is a wonderful thing.

It should be done in every city

in the nation."

Townspeople raised money

to send King to Washington, D.C.

King got Kansas lawmaker Ed Rees

excited about his idea.

Rees presented King's idea

to other U.S. lawmakers.

They agreed that the country needed

a way to thank all its veterans.

Thousands of women and men served

in wartime and peacetime to keep others free.

They needed to be noticed too.

In 1954, lawmakers voted
on Armistice Day again.
This time, they changed
the holiday's name to Veterans Day.
Two more soldiers were buried
in the tomb.
One soldier had died
during World War II.
The other had died in the Korean War.
The tomb was renamed
the Tomb of the Unknowns.
Veterans Day showed American pride
in servicepeople from all its wars.
The day also celebrated
the peace veterans brought.

The new name was not the last change
to the holiday.
In 1968, a law passed
making Veterans Day
the fourth Monday in October.
With no work or school on the holiday,
Americans could have a long weekend
to celebrate Veterans Day.
But several states refused
to change the date.
November 11 was the date
the armistice was signed.
It meant something special
to people in these states.
By 1978, national lawmakers agreed.
They returned Veterans Day
to November 11.

Since then, people in the United States
have found other ways
to honor veterans.
Post offices have sold stamps
honoring women in the armed forces.
Lawmakers have had statues
and other memorials built.
The memorials show veterans
from different wars.

One statue shows marines
raising the American flag
after a battle in World War II.
Another lists names of servicepeople
who died in the Vietnam War.
Americans fought the war in Vietnam
from 1965 to 1973.

In 1984, a soldier who died
during the Vietnam War was placed
in the Tomb of the Unknowns.
Now there were four soldiers
from four different wars.
Guards still keep watch at the tomb
around the clock.
Their watch honors all Americans
who gave their lives in war.
Many other countries find ways
to thank their veterans each year.
The names and celebrations may differ.
But most take place on November 11,
just like in the United States.

Canada and Australia call their holiday
Remembrance Day.
On that day, people remember
servicepeople who died.
Some people from Canada
wear red poppy flowers.
The poppies make them think
of veterans who died in poppy fields
of Europe during World War I.

Great Britain is another country
that celebrates Remembrance Day.
People go to church.
They march in parades.
Some lay poppies at memorials
of World War I.
Others stand silent for two minutes
at eleven o'clock.
This is their way to honor
those who lost their lives in wars.

In the United States, Veterans Day
will always be special.
The day tells millions
of women and men in the armed forces
that their work for peace is important.
Veterans use the day to think about
their time in the armed forces.
And Americans everywhere
use the day to thank them.

What Can You Do on Veterans Day?

Families find different ways to celebrate peace and honor veterans. Here are some things you can do for Veterans Day.

- Join your town's parade.
- Invite a serviceperson or veteran to talk with your class at school.
- Write a story about a veteran you know.
- Visit a veteran you know who needs help with chores or wants to talk.
- Write to a pen pal in the armed forces.
- Fly a flag outside your home.
- Sing songs that show pride in the United States, such as "My Country 'Tis of Thee."
- Color a flag to wave in a parade or hang in your room.
- Send a thank you card to someone in the armed forces.
- Visit a veterans' memorial or museum.
- Put on a play about Veterans Day.
- Place flowers on a soldier's grave.
- Make a list of things you can do to make a more peaceful world.

Important Dates

1918—World War I ends at eleven o'clock on November 11.

1919—President Woodrow Wilson names November 11 Armistice Day.

1921—An unknown soldier from World War I is buried in the Tomb of the Unknown Soldier.

1938—Lawmakers make Armistice Day a national holiday.

1941—The United States enters World War II. The war ends in 1945.

1950—The Korean War is fought. It ends in 1953.

1953—Ed King leads the people of Emporia, Kansas, to celebrate the first Veterans Day honoring veterans of all U.S. wars.

1954—Lawmakers change the name of the national holiday from Armistice Day to Veterans Day.

1958—An unknown soldier from World War II and one from the Korean War are buried in the Tomb of the Unknowns.

1968—Lawmakers change the date of Veterans Day to the fourth Monday in October.

1978—Congress returns Veterans Day to November 11.

1984—A Vietnam War veteran is buried in the Tomb of the Unknowns.

Websites about Veterans Day

Department of Veterans Affairs: VA Kids
http://www.va.gov/kids/k-5

Department of Veterans Affairs: Veterans Day
http://www1.va.gov/vetsday/

EnchantedLearning.com: Veterans Day Crafts
http://www.enchantedlearning.com/crafts/veterans/

Veterans Day School Play
http://www1.va.gov/pubaff/vetsday/vetplay.htm